# Secrets of a Garden City

# Secrets of a Garden City

## EXETER'S GARDENS IN WORDS AND PICTURES

*Text by*
GABRIEL LEVINE

*Paintings by*
DAVID EUSTACE

CORYLUS PRESS

First published 1990 by Corylus Press
53 Thornton Hill, Exeter EX4 4NR

© in the illustrations David Eustace 1990
© in the text Gabriel Levine 1990

ISBN 0 9515715 0 8

Designed by Spangle Graphics, Exeter

Typeset in Great Britain by P&M Typesetting Ltd, Exeter
Printed in Great Britain by Sprint Print Co. Ltd, Exeter

# Foreword

I am delighted to introduce this very personal account of the gardens and municipal planting of Exeter. The views which David Eustace has chosen to paint are seldom the obvious ones, and some are completely unknown to the average citizen. Civic Society member Gabby Levine uses the paintings to illustrate important principles of landscape design. The interrelation of plants and their background has, for example, seldom been set forth more clearly than in the pictures in this book.

If some of the scenes have altered, even vanished, since they were painted it surely vindicates the concern shown by our members in guarding both the city's architectural heritage and its garden character. At least these scenes – most notably the creeper-clad shoring in Castle Street, demolished in 1989 – have been affectionately recorded here for all time.

*Hazel Harvey, Publications Secretary, Exeter Civic Society, 1990*

# Preface

THE very title of this book is intended to be a challenge to garden enthusiasts in Exeter, as well as an inspiration and a stimulus to the thousands of people who visit the city every year. How many admirers of the city's bedding schemes and hanging baskets would guess that the biggest circular display of summer bedding is set smack in the middle of the local prison? How many visitors know that the most atmospheric view of the Cathedral is gained from the grounds of the Bishop's Palace, 50 yards east of the Cloisters, and that these grounds resemble a great and very ancient monastery garden?

The text is built around the salient features of each garden as they would appear to the first-time visitor. On my own first visit to Exeter, in June 1984, I was offered a short-term appointment with the city's Parks Department. Undecided whether to accept, I took a stroll in Rougemont and immediately fell under its spell – much of the work involved cataloguing the garden plants of Northernhay and Rougemont. During my tenure of the post, I was impressed not just by the outstanding horticultural status of these two parks, but by the contrast of garden styles to be found in a small area of the city centre. Thus was born the idea for a book about gardens that deserve to be known by a far wider public.

*G.L. 1989*

# Courtyard of the Bishop of Crediton  *10 Cathedral Close*

HALF-WAY DOWN Cathedral Close a covered passage leads into the most tempting town garden in Exeter. One peep – a discreet one – is enough to confirm the mystical yet somehow very human and tangible quality of this courtyard's 500 year-old history.

Built in the fourteenth or fifteenth century for a religious community, the courtyard's hall-house was later occupied by clergy at a time when up to 40 services a day were held in the Cathedral, and 100 priests lived in lodgings nearby. The house has only been a bishop's residence since the 1940s and is on a relatively humble scale. In its early days both yard and buildings must have been as down-to-earth as scores of others, with hens scratching around the hooves of carriage horses and pigs under the same roof as an archdeacon.

Some remnant of this domestic ambience still seems to mingle with the courtyard's ecclesiastical dignity – and is reflected by the daughter of the house and her drollish little friend in our painting. David Eustace has set the scene in the Edwardian period, when the overall appearance of house and yard had probably been unchanged for two or three centuries. Indeed, apart from a new roof and a window or two, architectural details and the quadrangle furnishings remained exactly like this until the end of the last war, narrowly escaping bomb damage in 1942. (The cast-iron moulding on top of the pump was stolen in 1986; its wooden pent-roof disappeared several years earlier.)

Hydrangeas in tubs and bay trees in pots are no longer grown here, but the remaining plants in the courtyard still match its spirit of durable quaintness. One subject follows another into bloom with Japanese simplicity. A species fuchsia, laden with pendant gems in summer and autumn, rambles in one corner. Winter jasmine cheers us with yellow flowers from November to February in another. Every May or June, for the last 200 years at least, wisteria festoons the wall with clouds of dusky mauve.

It is then that this sequestered quadrangle holds its greatest magic. It is worth making a pilgrimage to behold. A courtyard we have perhaps visited in an opium-induced vision, or half-remember from some childhood picture-book.

# Bishop's Palace Garden *Palace Gate*

THE fictitious peacock in this picture looks perfectly at home, and conveys the enchantment sometimes experienced by visitors to this semi-formal arrangement of gravel paths, box hedges and sculptured lawn. Few gardens are blessed with a lawn of such evenness of colour and texture, and even fewer display one level flowing down to another so soothingly.

Although the Palace dates from 1224, the early history of the garden is not recorded; but its lavish scale, like that of the episcopal residence itself, bespeaks the tremendous wealth and temporal power of the pre-Reformation bishops. A bishop of Exeter in the fourteenth century lived with all the grandeur of an earthly prince. His extensive household, in addition to a marshal and chamberlain, included clerks, chaplains, esquires, valets, bakers, stud-grooms, beer-brewers, messengers, page-boys, pig-keepers, hen-keepers, and endless serving-men. Coffers overflowed with gold rings and silver goblets. Enormous quantities of almonds, aniseed, cochineal and saffron (38lbs) were stored in the garderobe. Seventeen horses were stabled in the Great Courtyard. Even the greyhounds had silk slips with silver ornaments. A peacock would hardly be out of place among these symbols of Plantagenet luxury.

Domestic arrangements at the Palace had become hopelessly out-of-date by the twentieth century and more than one bishop had to take up residence in a private house. Some people still remember the period when the grounds were effectively open to the public while the Palace was occupied by the Ministry of Pensions. This arrangement ended in 1953, and since then the garden has been an integral and much-loved part of the Bishop's family home.*

The episcopal staff now consists of one secretary, a part-time domestic chaplain and a part-time chauffeur. A single gardener, provided by the Church Commissioners, keeps the lawn in top condition. Its surface of soft molten emerald is the perfect setting for the copper beeches and other trees that complete the satisfaction of this serene and classically English scene.

* Although the garden is private Bishop Thompson kindly allows guides from Exeter City Council to conduct tours of the Palace grounds at specific times. Telephone Exeter (0392) 265862 for details. The Bishop regrets that he is unable to admit visitors at other times.

## Garden Walkway *Rear of 1-10 Southernhay West*

THE merits of this walkway as a piece of landscape planning have been debated since 1975. Those who regard the scheme as too radical for its setting would probably dismiss our illustration as a romanticised interpretation. Some painterly tricks *have* been used to bring different hues into harmony, but the changes are subtle, and the picturesque quality of this portrait – essentially accurate in form and nearly so in colour – proves how well the scheme has matured as a planting composition.

The idea of a garden-bordered public walk alongside this stretch of city wall was put forward in 1949, but 26 years passed by before the backyards of the Southernhay terrace were cleared away and the proposal taken up. The good scale of the planting, devised by landscape architect Michael Oldham, results from an understanding that ample size means fewer things. A limited number of easy-care ground covers with coarse texture rightly dominate the beds, and express a relationship with clumps of large-leaved shrubs on the lawn, and with the canopies of mature trees which overhang the Roman wall from its ramparts inside the Bishop's Palace garden. Isolation of the weeping birch makes the most of its shape – and of the sentimental *tristesse* this shape evokes.

The mirror pools along the east boundary raised some eyebrows at first, but their terraced edges effectively merge the neo-Romanesque façade of new offices above them into the garden. Although the council intended to plant the pools with irises, hybrid water-lilies, double marsh marigolds, arrowhead, club-rushes and even water-chestnuts, this mix of deep water and marginal species proved difficult to establish, and the surface is usually covered by a green blanket of duckweed. When the pools are clear, however, their reflected light leads the eye straight to the eighteenth-century building which dominates the background with unassuming authority. Every aspect of the scene seems to flatter this edifice, with its grey stucco walls and dormer windows set in a lead-sheeted roof.

The scheme's wiggly path has always been a focus of attention. It may have an intriguing snake-like momentum in this view from the south, but looks decidedly contrived from the other end. Here the pedestrian, having descended the steps from Cathedral Close, is forced to check a natural tendency to continue walking in the same line. Even outright supporters of originality in landscape design expect ease of use, and if this path is the one jarring note in a scheme which otherwise fits so pleasingly into the surroundings, it only affirms the old principle that there is nothing wrong with a straight path in a straight setting.

# Rougemont Gardens

ROUGEMONT is an exciting place for gardeners, offering two borders of ornamental maples and a rockery where choice alpines, popular favourites, miniature bulbs and decidedly off-beat subjects jostle in romantic abandon. The backwaters of the long border harbour exotic shrubs long since forgotten by the park gardeners. These include Carolina allspice (*Calycanthus floridus*), with its curious maroon flowers and fragrant wood, and the Brazilian fruit salad tree (*Feijoa sellowiana*), which in hot countries produces a delicious guava-like fruit. But Rougemont is a people's garden and is loved just as deeply by those who don't know a pansy from a peony as by the erudite plantsman.

This study of sunlight falling into the great ditch of Rougemont Castle suggests why people, as well as squirrels, prefer Rougemont to Northernhay. It's a friendly garden, with an open centre, plenty of young trees, and not too many mature ones. It gives a comforting feeling which is strongest near Athelstan's Tower. The view from here – down into the great ditch and over the lovely dumpling-shaped hills to the south-east – probably combines with an awareness of a retreat inside the tower to gratify some basic animal instinct. We feel secure in places which have both a *prospect* over surrounding country – where we can see our prey, and a *refuge* – where we can hide from enemies.

Furthermore, the crumbling military defences in Rougemont tell more intimately of their great antiquity than they do over the wall in Northernhay. The name itself, *rouge mont*, has a Norman ring that resounds down the ages like a call to arms.

The trend from dedicated plantsmanship to a more basic style of upkeep, discernable in parts of Northernhay, has not touched the more solid charm of Rougemont. It never made particular claim to being a landscaped botanical collection. A garden as lovely as this, which can be relied on to soothe and bewitch us, sequestered enough for nuthatches to nest in, where young girls gather a feast of wild strawberries in June, a garden safe enough, indeed, to dream *in*, and romantic enough to dream *of* – such a garden needs no justification other than its existence.

# Northernhay Gardens

A FEW paces from Rougemont's cosy stronghold lie the sweeping lawns and exhilarating views of Northernhay. Considered as parts of a single park, divided by Castle precincts and Roman wall, the two gardens complement each other perfectly. The prospect and refuge components of a successful landscape are better integrated in Rougemont, and its layout discloses more unexpected features in a smaller area. But for those who think that intimate corners are missing from the grander garden, Mr Eustace has a surprise – a veritable lair of green velvet, immediately inside the gateway at Northernhay Place.

The large-leaved rather tropical foliage (under which many a vow must have been made and broken) belongs to a foxglove tree, part of Northernhay's impressive compendium of exotic plants. The placing of slim conifers in the drab flatness of a heather bed is typical of a somewhat haphazard style which gives the garden almost as much character as Rougemont.

From this point curving greens form the axis of an ornamental promenade, leading to a flamboyant memorial to the dead of World War I. With its valiant heroes in bronze, and an exultant female figure trampling a headstrong dragon and offering laurels to heaven, the memorial forms for most people the visual image that represents Northernhay Gardens. From Queen Street it culminates a tree-lined vista, dramatic enough to satisfy even Renaissance canons of garden design.

Although of long-standing repute as a plantsman's garden, Northernhay has borne the same retrenchment of skilled men as other public parks. Some of the banks plunging down to the station carry little else save large tracts of spotted laurel and winter heliotrope. But for every old shrubbery where good plants are choked by less worthy ones, a new border of flowering shrubs has been made somewhere else, or a bay in the overgrown rockery cleared and filled with garden alpines. A planting of hybrid azaleas, on a steep bank near the bandstand, is the latest stage in the redemption of Northernhay. Modern shrub borders are frequently enlivened when gaps are filled with some of the best new varieties available.

## X-Rings Garden *H.M. Prison, New North Road*

EXETER prison contains a whole series of garden features in addition to these beds of brilliant flowers. Other surprises include a honeysuckle trellis, lavish roses, dahlias good enough for a horticultural show, and a couple of seaside shrubs (*Coronilla glauca* and a choice hebe) not even found in the connoisseur's borders of Northernhay.

Most prisoners are exercised once a day here in the concentric circles of the X-Rings ('X' for exercise). The main group of up to 50 convicts come out at 11 am and perambulate for one hour. The severe trim endured at least twice-yearly by the weeping willow at the centre of the Rings is fraught with meaning: it allows officers to keep inmates under constant observation. 'E' men, known for escape attempts, and 'Rule 43' men, at risk of attack from other prisoners because of the nature of their offences, are aired in a closed yard surrounded by three- and four-storey buildings.

The grounds are tended by a civilian gardener assisted by two inmates of low escape risk. These men, who put in some 16,000 bedding plants each year, claim that most convicts are indifferent to the prison gardens. One wonders, however, what effect a mass of salvias, lobelias and French marigolds has on a human being in captivity. What effect does the passionate beauty of dahlias, or the romantic languor of roses, have on the spirit of a man awaiting trial? Is it too fanciful to imagine him drawing in great draughts of delicious hope?

The X-Rings garden was probably installed at the behest of a Victorian prison governor; most of the buildings are in the institutional style of the last century. The narrow building in the centre background, aptly window-less, is the old execution chamber – the 'topping shop'. The last hanging was of Gordon Trenoweth in 1943. Charlotte Bryant, who murdered her husband with a mug of poisoned Oxo in the hope of enjoying a life of bliss with her gypsy lover, was dispatched here in 1936.

The pit of the execution chamber is now used as a flour store for the prison kitchens. A small burial ground nearby, containing a dozen bodies of hanged prisoners in unmarked graves is, in summer, bright with asters, pelargoniums and ten-week stocks.

# Civic Centre *Paris Street*

IF there is such a thing as a dominant twentieth-century style in landscape gardening, the planting outside the Civic Centre is one of the best examples of it in Devon. It was designed by Chris Weighill in 1972, when he was half-way through a remarkable 25-year reign as Superintendent of Parks and Cemeteries.

The modernity of the scheme is economically justified by its modest requirements for skilled upkeep, achieved mainly by the replacement of traditional lawn with ground-covering plants. Its artistry works through an *apparently* free use of contrasting shapes and contours. In fact all the dominant subjects are meticulously placed in relationship to each other and to the building.

Execution of the design shows a complete mastery of the principle of using ground cover – not just functionally to smother weeds and keep maintenance to a minimum, but also, in combination with slightly taller shrubs of diverse texture (*Potentilla*, *Berberis*, *Hypericum* 'Hidcote', *Senecio* 'Sunshine'), to form a neutral background of 'filler' material. This holds the entire planting together and enables it to carry safely the more positive shapes of the columnar trees.

Although characterised by the juxtaposition of texture and mass, rather than by colour and the display of specimens, the scheme does use a couple of Japanese cherries to breath-taking effect in spring – namely 'Shirotae', laden with snow-white blossom on horizontal branches. A considerable area, too, is given over to shrubs which carry masses of yellow flowers from June to September. This blends in with the concrete background and forms a setting for pleasing colour harmonies on a smaller scale, such as the carmine of *Spiraea* 'Anthony Waterer' behind the mauve of lavender. Some seasonal bedding, with red salvias of potentially strident brilliance, is dovetailed into the tail-end of the planting with supreme confidence.

## Zigzag Bed  *Bus and Coach Station*

MOST visitors to Exeter are immediately impressed by the opulence of floral decoration in the city centre. A profusion of busy lizzies and petunias, displayed on balconies and shop-front ledges for a full quarter-of-a-mile above the main streets, helped the city win the European Entente Florale competition in 1981. Of more interest as a design, however, is the blazing zigzag at the Bus Station in Paris Street.

Bedding-out was one of the keynotes of the Victorian private garden. The annual routine of placing greenhouse-raised, brilliantly-flowered plants in outdoor beds was taken up with particular zest by municipal gardeners at the turn of the century. But when floral clocks and coats of arms had become the stock-in-trade of every parks superintendent, a new generation of garden inspirers had popularised the herbaceous border and the flowering shrub garden. They scorned bedding, not because it was ostentatious and artificial, but because it did not fit happily into the surrounding landscape.

The difficulty of using ribbon-style bedding in a grass setting is demonstrated in Southernhay today. Its dazzling colours look slightly incongruous in the overall garden scene. The zigzag bed, on the other hand, benefits enormously from its isolation in a closer setting. Blazing salvias are deliberately played off against a neutral background of paving. Accents of hare's tail grass, and an edge of bluish-grey helichrysum, complete an impeccable colour scheme and provide just the right amount of 'finish'. Even the National Express symbol figures in the perfect setting of this refreshing little masterpiece of horticultural art.

Exeter Bus and Coach Station, with its sensible layout and magnificent screen of ornamental shrubs, won the Best Kept Bus Station award in 1986. The prize, £100 worth of rose bushes of a new floribunda called 'Beautiful Britain', was planted in the points of the zigzag later that year. Its pinkish-orange blooms, while spoiling the purity of the original design, at least extend the flowering season into October and November, by which time the summer bedders have been discarded and replaced by hardy subjects for spring display.

## Garden of St Olaves Court Hotel  *Mary Arches Street*

ALTHOUGH the grounds of St Olaves Court Hotel share their elusive charm with other old-world, walled gardens of ecclesiastical origin in Exeter, this is the only one furnished with a traditional ornamental pond. It sets the whole mood of the garden and releases the onlooker into that languid world where there is room for the play of imagination as well as for the actual eye. The little girl, hypnotised by nothing more than the passage of time; the model waiter, straight out of a cheap novel; gorgeous red roses in half-shadow – all these are imbued with the balm of water and could have been stolen from the garden's subconscious memories.

While girl and waiter may gaze across the pool through the medium of astral projection, everything else in the painting is a faithful reproduction of the scene as it was before recent alterations. The garden had belonged to the rectory of St Olave's Church until Donald Clarke bought the whole property – garden, rectory, and its adjoining church house – for conversion to a hotel in 1982. Both houses were built in 1827 for James Golsworthy, a local contractor who ran a piped-water business using supplies pumped up from the River Exe. During the cholera epidemic in 1832 he became the most sought-after man in town, supplying poor households at no charge as dead bodies piled up and everyone clamoured for clean water.

The authorities later rewarded Golsworthy's benevolence by arranging for the fountain in his garden pool to be connected to a free supply of water from the Longbrook spring. According to the sale documents of 1982, they also eased the water rates for this property 'in perpetuity'. But no regal jet of water shoots into the air in our picture because it was painted in 1986, by which time the fountain tap was firmly turned off. The Clarkes had cheerfully run the fountain, now connected to the mains, for six months before South West Water explained that the Golsworthy concession had been withdrawn and the rates were due. Then, in 1987, the pool itself disappeared under rubble when builders restored the Hotel's rectory wing. The new pond installed later, however, has an exquisite little fountain whose water is recirculated by a submerged pump. The refreshing sound of settling spray now consoles us for new paving laid up to the pool's edge, and the consequent loss of some well-placed waterside perennials.

# Southernhay Court *Southernhay Gardens*

THIS garden is a perfect demonstration of landscape art – the art of using plant material to compose outdoor pictures. It was designed by Brenda Taylor in 1976, and is one of several schemes in Southernhay Gardens, the campus-style office complex which stretches from Westernway to Southernhay East.

The silver birch trees, which Mrs Taylor has placed with exquisite judgement near the centre of her garden picture, have an elegance and grace that not only soothe the hard lines of the surrounding buildings, but positively flatter them – especially when contrasted with the heavy boughs and sombre foliage of the evergreen oaks shading the Court's western approach.

There are two native birches in Britain, but the one known as downy birch, which grows so abundantly in the Scottish Highlands and often springs up from wind-sown seed in gardens, is rarely, if ever, planted for ornament. It lacks the narrow crown and long pendulous branchlets which give silver birch its feminine poise. The trunk of the silver has a much clearer tone than the downy, and benefits from all the play of sun and wind it gets in a garden. In thick woods the bark is often marred by greenish scum.

Although it works so well as a picturesque scene, this garden is not, somehow, one in which an onlooker is tempted to linger, and it would be less suitable as a private plot. This is one of the drawbacks of a style which relies entirely on landscape planting for its effects. The ground cover, essential in unifying the composition as a piece of scenery seen from a modest distance, does little at close quarters to calm the slightly unsettling presence of the office blocks which enclose the Court. Rose of Sharon, in such quantity, would be too coarse for a private garden of this size. Even the grass has an exclusively pictorial role, helping the eye appreciate the hue of bricks and the beauty of trees.

Southernhay Court then, while not a place for afternoon tea or a game of croquet, is a model of architectural enhancement. No one expects it to contain the mystery and romance of gardens like St Olaves Court, whose effect, although still dependent on good design, is intimately linked to spiritual qualities acquired over very many years.

# Garden of William Pollard & Co. Ltd *Southernhay Gardens*

IN 1976 the land at the rear of Pollard's printing works was a dismal piece of ground without a worthwhile plant. Two goats – Billy and Nancy – had kept the grass down for several years. Then Bracey Gardens Ltd were asked to submit a plan to flatter the unusual features of the site. Mr Bracey designed and installed a modern garden which followed his brief to the letter.

Some may think the layout of this garden is far from modern. Certainly its style is very different from the landscape planting in Southernhay Gardens, where trees and shrubs have been arranged solely to tie the buildings into a pleasant setting. Pollard's, by contrast, is virtually a private garden, seemingly carved out of the flanking terrain of concrete and brick, ramps, drives and fortress-like offices.

The word *modern*, in gardening at least, can be applied to any style which has evolved since World War I. This garden resembles nothing more than one of the 'new' designs for a small uphill property in the United States in the 1930s. Although modernism is usually perceived in terms of flowing lines and unsymmetrical relationships, the good modern designer does not discard symmetry in a regular site.

Others would argue that Bracey has only modified old-style symmetry by giving it some of the neatness and crispness we associate with modern art. Does it matter whether we classify the garden as traditional or modern? What is important is that he has worked from principals rather than 'feel'. In reality the layout is not that symmetrical; but its *illusion* of symmetry gives the whole scene an occult theatricality. These machine minders in white coats could be androids about to witness a blood sacrifice on the platform of a Mayan temple.

The garden is further distinguished by its use of enclosure as an element of design. The pair of solid Leyland cypresses just over the boundary wall, and the variegated thujas closely ranked in their own company on the inside boundary, are perfectly assimilated into the composition. They draw the eye from flowers and foliage behind the terrace, and focus it squarely on the drama of thirteen steps crossing an empty lawn. They give the garden a compelling individuality rare in modern planting.

## Herbaceous Border *Bury Meadow*

THIS border of hardy perennials was only planted in 1984. By its second season it was strong enough to evoke the haunting beauty of those old-fashioned flower borders which were once one of the glories of the English garden. The classic herbaceous border, with its informal drift planting and bold masses of harmonised colour, gave a succession of bloom from early summer to early autumn. It also provided cut flowers for the house, and was perhaps the most cherished feature in an ideal garden for the first 50 years of this century. Herbaceous perennials are still grown in nearly every garden today, but usually take a subordinate role alongside other classes of plants, including small flowering shrubs.

None of the flowers in the section of border shown here would have been out of place in the garden of a country house in, say, the peaceful days of 1912. Pre-eminent among them is that divine aristocrat, the delphinium. Its columns of radiant blue stand before the soft yellow candelabras of the biennial mullein, *Verbascum olympicum*. The yarrow at the front is 'Cerise Queen', a 1930s variety only slightly richer than its Edwardian counterpart. Just behind is a drift of ox-eye chamomile, *Anthemis tinctoria*; it was purchased as 'Kelwayi' – a true 1912-er, virtually unknown today. The reddish-purple spikes under the tree belong to a variety of purple loosestrife, hardly different from the lovely wild plant which grows by the Exe.

A liberal planting of that bonny old stager, the sweet william, is a recent addition to the border. Although not mingling happily with perennials of totally different habit, its use as a reserve measure to hide bare ground is welcome. Indeed, it is a major task keeping a border of this size – 100 yards long by 6 yards deep – clear of perennial weeds and furnished with enough plants to give continuity of flower.

The border was conceived with praiseworthy enthusiasm. But its future, especially with the prospect of private tendering round the corner, is uncertain. Perhaps, one day, the kind of dedicated after-care for which the council are renowned will make Bury Meadow a picture-book success. Then it will be chock-full of bloom, giving not the steady blaze which blocks of tender bedders produce, but a thrilling sequence of glowing harmonious colour in the true style of English border gardening.

## Pinces Gardens *Near Alphington Road, St Thomas*

IF there is one park in Exeter worth visiting for a single feature alone it is Pinces Gardens, with its 45-yard long pergola of mature wisteria. Few who have seen it in late spring are likely to forget the sight, if sumptuous arrangement of gorgeous blossom means anything to them.

Most pergolas in England today are solid affairs with brick or stone piers and timber cross-beams. Their style is inspired by the partly-shaded terraces of the Italian Riviera, where, from the late Renaissance onwards, they have commonly been used for growing vines and ripening grapes. The primitive appearance of the Pinces version seemingly owes more to the pleached alleys of our Tudor ancestors. It was already a famous landmark in St Thomas in the 1880s. Over the next 30 years the idea of displaying climbing plants above a walkway was taken up by the best garden architects in England, and pergolas on classic Riviera lines appeared in the grounds of country houses all over the Home Counties.

In the nineteenth century Pinces Gardens was a plant nursery renowned for its vast glasshouses packed with seductive orchids, gardenias and rare palms. It was still a nursery when the council bought the property – pergola thrown in – in 1912 and converted it to a pleasure ground.

The typical pergola of that period, built by Sir Edwin Lutyens for a Gertrude Jekyll garden, was an architectural device linking the main house with a structural feature in the garden, such as a summer house. Our pergola does not have such an obvious destination. Nevertheless, its setting amongst formal lawns and yew hedges with flat tops and bulging sides does echo another Jekyllian taste, not for the Renaissance gardens of Italy, but for the good old topiary gardens of northern England and Scotland.

Wisteria blossom emits a delicious perfume and the very idea of walking beneath it has an irresistible romantic force. Inspired by this Olympian mood, David Eustace uses the pergola to enframe a pair of twins in a voluptuous tunnel of sisterly love.

# City Wall *Bailey Street*

TWO faces of Exeter are revealed in this apparently mundane street scene. The back end of Boots – all Flemish bond brickwork and metal-framed windows with concrete sills and lintels – is typical of the functional style in which Exeter was rebuilt after the devastation of 1942, while the section of city wall opposite carries the romance of Exeter's 2000 years of history. But rarely are things quite as they seem, and the quaint metal staircase and door, which seem to echo with the footsteps of the past and suggest, at the very least, secret passages into a Cromwellian stronghold, were built after the last war and lead to the beer garden of the Royal British Legion Club. Even the wall itself has no Roman core at this point, although its base is Norman and the facework looks as mellowed as other stretches at least 700 years old.

The postwar buildings – rather stark at first alongside some of the medieval treasures which survived Hitler's bombs – at least have a comprehensible scale. It is precisely their lack of stylistic tricks which will make them classical in the future. The city's defences, built by the Romans and Normans as an invincible stone barrier with a drop of 30 to 40 feet on the inside, now regarded as beautiful in their simplicity, were, at the time, as staid and true to the materials of the period as our 1950s department stores.

A subconscious sympathy with this reasoning has, perhaps, made Mr Eustace pair one artless teenager of today with a companion so homely she could be her counterpart from 1952. If the girls are co-ordinates in a strangely pleasing composition, and represent a kind of postwar sleepy plainness, then the focus in this composition is the little tree with its mantle of off-white blossom. Something about its bandy trunk, its configuration of branches in a not-quite balanced canopy, give it an awkward grace and self-possession which is absolutely right for this setting. It becomes conspicuous again in autumn with splendid clusters of bright red berries which last until April.

The species, *Cotoneaster frigidus*, is rarely seen in a street. It is not on the short list of trees which are selected over and over again for planting along roadsides because their habit is considered appropriate. But this dinky tree blends into its full-blooded background and soothes away any potential architectural clash with the newish building opposite. Fortuitous scenes like this contribute as much to the garden character of Exeter as do the flower-beds and landscape schemes along the main streets.

## Wooden Shoring *Castle Street*

THIS ravishing display of autumn colour has an unusual history. In 1961 there was a dispute between the city and the county, as to whether Bailey Street should be shut to traffic or remain open. The county won and the street was kept open, but a listed building at the end of Castle Street had to be pulled down to increase visibility for approaching traffic. Then Mr Hay, who runs the ecclesiastical suppliers where men of the cloth can buy anything from a parson's pocketbook to a bishop's mitre, insisted that the exposed wall of his premises be properly buttressed. Ten years later the original shorings began to fall down and were replaced with props of thicker dimension.

When the city Parks Department decided to screen these massive baulks of timber with Virginia creeper, more than one plant, after being coaxed into rooting in the compacted rubble at the base of the wall, was hacked down by marauding vandals. Once the creeper got away there was no stopping it. Self-clinging in a similar manner to ivy, but far outstripping it in speed of growth, it covered the end wall and threw a mask of luxuriant wreaths over the timbers themselves. A downright utilitarian structure – almost medieval in its guileless strength – was transformed into a striking piece of backstreet scenery.

The vine used is the Asian species, *Parthenocissus tricuspidata*; this is more vigorous than the true Virginia creeper (*P. quinquefolia*) from the USA, and has replaced it as the most important climbing plant in British horticulture. Nothing is more effective or beautiful, but it does need sedulous pruning on fine buildings. Our creeper is only trimmed on the side walls, and sanguine garlands several feet in length hang from the timbers in autumn.

Autumn colour is extremely variable and the Castle Street vine, even at its zenith in October, is usually less stunning than other Virginia creepers in town. Its crimson is less pure and more purplish, although a mass of foliage may turn russet for a few days, and at least a few small leaves glow like garnets seen against the light. The azure sky in our picture, beneath which a couple of barristers head for the Crown Courts in Rougemont Castle, is not too fanciful either. It suggests a nip in the air and forbodes a time when a brisk wind, or an early frost, will dismantle this bonfire of colour in a few days.

# Acknowledgements

GABBY Levine would like to thank the many friends who have helped him, in particular Julie Hoare and Dorothy Haston, and also all the people who have supplied information about the scenes in this book.

The illustration of the Bishop's Courtyard is after a painting by E. W. Haslehust in *Beautiful England: Exeter*, published by Blackie & Son Limited.

The publishers wish to express their gratitude for generous financial support from Mr Norman Langdon, chairman of St Bridget Nurseries Ltd, leading suppliers of plants to the whole of the Exeter region; from Sclater's Victoria Nurseries, who have been selling rock plants and bulbs in Exeter Market for over a century; from St Olaves Court Hotel, the privately-owned country house hotel off Mary Arches Street; from P&M Typesetting Ltd, Exeter; from William Pollard & Co. Ltd, system form printers, also of Exeter; and from the Alec French Partnership of Bristol, one of whose architects designed the planting in Southernhay Court.

We are very pleased indeed to acknowledge a leading donation from Mr Tom French, director of Teign Valley Nursery (Christow) and of the garden accessories shop in Sidwell Street, long renowned for its high standard of personal service.